Enactments

EDITED BY RICHARD SCHECHNER

To perform is to imagine, represent, live and enact present circumstances, past events and future possibilities. Performance takes place across a very broad range of venues from city streets to the countryside, in theatres and in offices, on battle-fields and in hospital operating rooms. The genres of performance are many, from the arts to the myriad performances of everyday life, from courtrooms to legislative chambers, from theatres to wars to circuses.

ENACTMENTS encompasses performance in as many of its aspects and realities as there are authors able to write about them.

ENACTMENTS will include active scholarship, readable thought and engaged analysis across the broad spectrum of performance studies.

KADDISH

Pages on Tadeusz Kantor

Jan Kott

EDITED BY PIOTR KŁOCZOWSKI

TRANSLATED BY JAKOB ZIGURAS

LONDON NEW YORK CALCUTTA

The editor and the publisher would like to specially acknowledge Maria Kantor and Dorota Krakowska for sharing photographs from Tadeusz Kantor's family collection for this edition.

Seagull Books, 2020

© Miachel Kott, 2020; Lidia Beryer, 2020
Afterword © Piotr Kłoczowski, 2020
English translation © Jakob Ziguras
Photographs from Kantor family collection © Maria Kantor
and Dorota Krakowska
Photographs of theatre props © Janusz Podlecki

ISBN   978 0 8574 2 748 9

British Library Cataloguing-in-Publication Data
A catalogue record for this book is available from the British Library

Typeset by Seagull Books, Calcutta, India
Printed and bound by Chicago Distribution Center, Ill., USA

CONTENTS

Tadeusz Kantor

Born 6 April 1915, in Wielopole Skrzyńskie
Died 8 July 1990, in Krakow

FIGURE 1. The parish church in Wielopole Skrzyńskie,
dedicated to the Most Holy Virgin Mar.

FIGURE 2. Helena Kantor née Berger, the mother of Tadeusz Kantor

FIGURE 3. Marian Kantor, Helena Kantor née Berger, Stanisław Berger, from before 1914.

FIGURE 4. A photograph of recruits from the Austrian army. Marian Kantor, the father of Tadeusz Kantor, is the first from the left in the front row.

THE THEATRE OF DEATH

The Dead Class, premiered on 15 November 1975, Galeria Krzysztofory, Krakow.

Where Are The Snows of Yesteryear?, premiered on 27 January 1979, Palazzo delle Esposizioni, Rome.

Wielopole, Wielopole, premiered on 23 June 1980, Teatro Regionale Toscano, Florence.

Let The Artists Die, premiered on 2 June 1985, Alte Giesserei Kabelmetall, Nuremburg.

I Shall Never Return, premiered on 23 April 1988, in Teatro Studio, Milan.

Today Is My Birthday, premiered on 10 January 1991, Théâtre Garonne, Toulouse.

He spoke a throaty French. He started
chatting with me in Hebrew and in Yiddish.
Once again, he made sure: 'Are you a Jew?'
He led me a few streets further to a small
private synagogue. In the vestibule stood a
cluster of women. Inside, on the left, there
was a long table. At the table sat men in
round hats and long kapotes. They ate and
drank. In the middle of that small room, two
huge candelabra burnt before tablets of the
commandments. On the right stood yet
another small candelabrum. In front of it, a
young man with an elongated face rocked
forward, at first slowly, then ever faster, then
still faster, till he was positively dizzying, and
called out what seemed to me to be always
the same words. I stopped before the burn-
ing candelabra and thought of my father and
of my mother, of my father's parents and of

my mother's parents. This was my prayer for the dead. On my left, men in hats ate and drank a festive Friday supper. On my right, the young Jew had now stopped rocking and stood motionless before his small candelabrum. In what other city would a stranger ask if I have said Kaddish for my father?

ESSENCES

In Tadeusz Kantor's *The Dead Class,* the dead return to their former places on school benches. Before the show begins, the benches are arranged on the stage, just in front of the chairs for the audience. On the benches sit mannequins of boys and girls. The dead sit down beside themselves, beside their former selves, beside the selves that once existed. There are two different 'classes', summoned from oblivion and called out by Kantor's memory (like a student, who is called upon to answer). The first is a class before their last exams, in a Galician gymnasium, in a small town of the Austro-Hungarian Empire, on the eve of the First World War. The second 'class', in Kantor's hallucinatory spectacle, is the dead—or, rather, the utterly gutted—ethos of that corner of the earth where Poles, Ukrainians and Jews had once lived alongside one another.

I saw *The Dead Class* for the first time only at the La MaMa theatre, in New York. When from the stage, beside the melody of the Viennese waltz, *François*, which drove the performance—rising to an almost deafening volume and falling to a whisper—there sounded for a moment Yiddish lullabies, I thought to myself that this theatre hall in the East Village is one of very few places in the world where one can find, among the audience, two, three or maybe even four people to whom those lullabies were sung once, in Yiddish, by a grandma or a mother. In them, the dead of Kantor are still living.

I saw Kantor's *Wielopole, Wielopole* at this same theatre, La MaMa, in the East Village, next to Second Avenue, where Polish restaurants serve Russian *pierogi*, while the Ukrainian ones serve *żurek* with Krakow-style sausage. This is also a theatre of the returning dead and of mannequins that are the doubles of the living. Or, one could say it in yet another way: namely, that, in Kantor's theatre, the living are the doubles of the mannequins. The living are the doubles of the dead, and this is probably the most important thing that Kantor has to say.

In *The Dead Class*, the theatrical vision—repeating itself persistently and having the physicality and obsessiveness of a nightmare—is a procession of the dead, returning in order to take a seat again on their school benches. In *Wielopole*, the vision—which, both in terms of image and of theme, organizes the show (in Kantor, image, theme and obsession, like a lump that hurts, like a Freudian trauma, are one and the same)—is contained in the faded photograph of seven recruits from the First World War, enlisted into the Austrian army. They stand at attention in their field uniforms, rifles with attached bayonets at their sides.

A photograph—and in this lies the art's singularity among all others—is a sign that something existed. Even faded it persists as a fact of memory. It continues as a trace. A photographic print—its once gleaming paper—is, in all its brittleness, more lasting than the human body. Throughout the great expanses of the world, and now almost without exception in much of Central Europe, this small piece of paper has often shown itself to be more enduring than houses of brick and concrete, than human dwellings with their entire contents. As Roland Barthes showed in *Camera Lucida*, the last of his books, published only after his death—a photograph is simultaneously time dead and time arrested. It is a sign of death, but a specific sign—a likeness; that which is dead, that which was, is rendered motionless; it *is*, it endures, submitted to the decomposition of cellulose. Kantor discovered at once the terror and the theatricality of a photograph of the dead.

In *Wielopole*, the recruits from the First World War have faded uniforms and pasty faces. They move like puppets. They are not only dead, they are exhumed. And in the final scene, after the Last Supper, to which all of the characters of this family drama have sat down, they will be thrown into a mass grave. Into this same mass grave will be thrown their naked mannequins/doubles. In *Wielopole, Wielopole*, the dramatis personae are the members of a family: a father, a mother, a grandma, four uncles, of whom one is a prelate, maternal and paternal aunts. The father is one of the recruits; the uncle-prelate, clad in a stole, will bind him with the mother in a marriage ceremony. The other recruits will rape the mother, still in her wedding dress. Her mannequin lies on the stage with legs spread wide. But already beforehand, in the wedding-photo scene, the bride moves like a puppet. The father/groom moves like a skeleton. The old-fashioned camera will transform into a machine gun. From the camera extends a tube like a barrel. All perish under gunfire.

In Kantor's theatre, the living have already long been corpses. The family history begins with the reconstruction of a room that once existed. 'Only we were absent from this room,' says one of the identical-twin uncles. The corpse of the uncle-prelate lies on a bed. A turn with a hand crank and the mattress flips over: on the bed, fastened with belts, lies the mannequin of the priest/prelate. In Kantor's theatre, objects—knocked out of their everydayness, deprived of their functions—serve as dramatic props. Kantor admits to a kinship with Marcel Duchamp ('reality can be presented only through reality'). In the late 1930s, during my youthful studies in Paris, I admired the surrealist iron with nails hammered into its base, or the violin of *Homage to Paganini*, tightly bandaged like a sprained hand. The destroyed iron and the bandaged violin have for a long time now been museum objects, like Duchamp's famous urinal.

In Kantor's theatre, props torment both bodies and imagination. However, in *Wielopole, Wielopole*, the mechanical cruelty, which almost always has in itself something of the macabre joke, is supplanted by terror. The family drama occurs during war time. As in Goya, terror requires no signature. Words are only a movement of the lips. To the accompaniment of a military march, which—like the waltz *François*, in *The Dead Class*—grows quiet, only to deafen us soon after, the corpses rise from the dead, in order to expire again a moment later.

Kantor terrifies us with an image. And, as in Goya's wartime cycle, Kantor's dramatic images, apart from their graphic cruelty, refer to signs that are the *arche* of terror and humiliation. This Christian *arche* of despair is the Son of God stretched upon the cross. A heavy wooden cross is dragged onto the stage on the arms of the uncle/prelate, who just a moment ago had blessed the recruits during a military parade. Passing through stations of the Lord's Passion, the recruits will liken themselves to the tormentors scourging Christ. One by one, the actors of the family drama will hang upon the cross: firstly the raped bride, lastly the prelate. Kantor's theatre, which began with the degradation of objects, becomes a blasphemy of the *sacrum*. Or, perhaps, the levelling in humiliation of *sacrum* and *profanum*. This final humiliation is death.

I call Kantor's theatre a theatre of essence. According to Sartre's famous definition, existence precedes essence. Existence is choices and games: moral, intellectual, social. Existence is freedom of choice. Essence is what remains of us. Essence is the human drama purified of accidents and of the illusion that it contains choices. Essence is trace. Like the impress of a crustacean on a stone, not yet completely washed away by water.

Everyman is a theatre of Christian essence. The drama is contained in a single question: Who will descend into the grave with you? The Dance of Death is also a theatre of essence, though in it, from the beginning, a suppressed laugh accompanied the terror. This renaissance Dance of Death is the key to Kantor's theatre. In every one of his shows, at least one of the characters is a figure of death. In *The Dead Class,* she was a camp follower; in *Wielopole,* it is one of the aunts. She has a rag in her hand. With it, she first washes the corpses and, then, wipes the floor of blood. Graves are traces of history. In the twentieth century, these are mass graves. 'Death transforms life into fate,' wrote Malraux. In Kantor's theatre, death wipes away the traces of itself with a wet rag, from which it then wrings water.

Shakespeare contains everything. In his work, there is also a theatre of essence. In *Macbeth*, Act 1, Scene 2, a messenger arrives from the battlefield: 'What bloody man is that? He can report, / As seemeth by his plight of the revolt / The newest state'. This messenger from the field of battle—half-naked and completely soaked in blood, without surname or name—is the unknown soldier, the very essence of history. I see this essence in Kantor's theatre.

In traditional Japanese theatre, the stage continues to be a liturgical place of sacrifice. The excellent anthropologist Masao Yamaguchi calls this the place of negation, where there occurs a meeting with death. But in opposition to the theatre of existence, in the liturgical theatre, death is not individual. In the theatre of essence, it is history that is mortal. Kantor, present/absent on the stage from the first to the last moment of the performance, stooped, always in the same black outfit and dark scarf, urging on his actors with a light, sometimes almost imperceptible, flick of the fingers—as if impatient

that all of this still takes so long—may perhaps appear as Charon, who takes the dead
across to that other shore. But Kantor not
only sees off the dead, he also calls them
back. In this theatre of the fading and
washed-away trace, Kantor—present on
the stage—is the memory of places and of
people. And this constitutes the uniqueness
and gravity of *The Dead Class* and of
Wielopole, Wielopole.

Nowy Sad, May 1982

FIGURE 5. A wheel from *The Return of Odysseus*.

IN MICKIEWICZ

In the evocation of that which is forgotten, torn out, burnt, by history—as in the drawing forth of what is forgotten in one's own, singular personal history—times and events are superimposed on one another and have their own continuity, their own errant chronology and affinities.

Some major or colonel of the German army, from the offensive of 1915, observes through field binoculars the ruins of the palace in Tuchanowicze. Suddenly, Mickiewicz appears behind his back; meanwhile, Maryla stands on the balcony of the burnt-out palace, in a white robe and with a rose-coloured ribbon. No, Maryla Wereszczakówna did not stand on the balcony, when Mickiewicz arrived at Tuchanowicze, for the first time, with Odyniec. It was in fact Odyniec who wrote down this account: 'On the armrests of two chairs, set up in the middle, there lay an ironing-board; on it there was a pile of collars and ladies' handkerchiefs, as well as a wide rose-coloured ribbon, in the process of being ironed. Already ironed and freshened for Sunday, a white dress hung in the doorway on a hinge. There was no one in the little room . . . .'

Amazing are the mysteries of memory, whether—and here I don't know which describes it best—it is personal or most deeply poetic. Maryla's white dress, 'on a hinge' in the doorway, returns, as if retained on a photographic plate, in the white dress of Zosia, laid 'on an armrest':

> . . . *disorder dear!*
> *Young were the little hands that threw*
> > *them here.*
> *Nearby, the white dress also, ready to*
> > *be worn*
> *fresh from the hanger, on a chair*
> > *undone.*

And so, it is always Wereszczakówna, even years later, in the Zosia of *Pan Tadeusz*:

> *The modest youth covered his squinting*
>   *eyes;*
> *he wished to say something, apologize,*
> *but only bowed, withdrawing; pained,*
>   *the maid*
> *cried out as would a child who wakes*
>   *afraid.*
> *The traveller, flustered, looked, but she*
>   *was gone.*
> *He left perplexed, feeling his heart beat*
>   *on*
> *Aloud . . .*

Places, faces, gestures, outfits—sometimes even the kettle in which the doctor's wife, Mrs Kowalska, brewed coffee for Mickiewicz—all are for a brief moment arrested and frozen, as if deprived of their own time and transported into other times, in which our own is also present when we participate in this ritual evocation of the dead.

In these images—immobilized, or
moving at a suddenly slowed tempo—there
is perhaps at times even more of Fellini than
of Proust. I am thinking of the black-and-
white sequences, recalled from childhood
memory, in Fellini's unforgettable *Amacord*.
The sensitivity of Rymkiewicz has in itself
something of the sudden and unexpected
inventiveness of the film camera: 'At the
sanatorium in Merano, Jadwiga Truhanowska
enters naked into the frame of the Röntgen
machine . . . .'

And who will dispute that this was 1881,
and so almost fifteen years before the inven-
tion of the Röntgen lamp? *The Magic
Mountain* also returns for a moment in this
tangle.[1] As does also the *życzka*, a woollen
ribbon used for lacing corsets, or as a garter.
This crimson ribbon returns three or four
times. At the very end, Karolina ties it above
her white-stockinged knee. In Rymkiewicz's

1 The untranslatable word *żmut*, which is also the title
of Jarosław Marek Rymkiewicz's book, means, roughly,
'a chaotic tangle of hair, ribbons or threads' and was used
by Poles living in Lithuania.

personal 'tangle', this crimson ribbon fulfils the function of Proust's madeleine. Where have they gone, the maidens with ribbons for garters?

Times are mixed together as in the Dantean *Purgatory*, because our dead—the dead beloved and the dead of the nation ('whether where the nation falls, or the lover dies . . .')—exist in the same timeless oblivion. And this is why, for me, in some deep and hidden manner, Rymkiewicz's *Tangle* comes close to Kantor's *The Dead Class* and *Wielopole, Wielopole*. These are different parts and different generations, within the burnt-out walls of now non-existent homesteads; but in both identically the country of the dead returns and, in this diaspora of Kantor's, different times also blend.

Stony Brook, August 1987

AT WHAT STATION?

I first attended the initial rehearsal at the Akademie der Künste. It was probably four or five days after Kantor's arrival in Berlin, with his last show. The benches rose upwards like an amphitheatre. The hall was filled with the old and young, as at a premier. For a moment, it seemed to me that I knew them all, that I had seen them all somewhere already, that these were still the same spectators of Kantor, as in New York's La MaMa, as in Milan.

On stage was the same Kantor, dressed in black. The one thing I cannot remember is whether, formerly, he also had the same white scarf. He also seemed to have a new hat, made of felt and softer. He had always seemed to me like Charon; but, this time, he celebrated the same ritual of hastening—as if he were in a rush that everyone should now, once and for all, depart—more gently than usual, with some rending sadness. As if he were bidding himself farewell.

In the depths of the stage there were four doors. And through these four doors, which opened and closed, there ran in a circling stampede, breathless, sometimes only briefly stopping, as if they chased or fled one another: the parish priest from Wielopole, with a cross, sweeping the stage with the tails of his cassock; a waiter with a carafe on a tray; two twin Hasidim; a charwoman with a huge bust that spilt out of her apron (the whole of her as if observed in Goya), wiping the floor with a rag and constantly—in this ceaseless rush of washing the floor and running to the waiter and the priest—also running up to Kantor, as if she were asking him about something. Then, an army orchestra appeared and disappeared through the middle door, in shakos and braided uniforms as if still from before the First World War. They played fiddles and lifted their legs high in a parade march. A little Jew, straight from Chagall, leapt out from somewhere and began conducting. The orchestra vanished through the door. The little Jew in the yarmulke continued, for a moment, to conduct in silence. Kantor shouted terribly at the sound engineer, who was hidden somewhere beyond the benches, beneath the ceiling.

I did not stay until the end of this rehearsal, but it seemed to me that I had grasped the principle of its movement. The figures appeared and disappeared, as on the clocks of Renaissance or Baroque churches or town halls, where saints or kings are often accompanied by Death bearing a scythe. Or as on elaborate music boxes, where the little figures—prancing and turning in a circle—are stubbornly accompanied by the same lively melody. The door opens and closes, characters appear and disappear; but, I had guessed already by the middle of the rehearsal that, at the end, the door would close on everyone, would close on Kantor's theatre, never again to open. And then I understood the words: 'I will never return here.'

Still before the performance had begun, tables and chairs were arranged on the stage, one upon the other as in a restaurant at dawn, before the first guests appear. A waiter with a napkin in hand was arranging the chairs and, with a yardstick, methodically measuring the distance between tables. He nudged the priest, who had fallen asleep on an empty table. Or, perhaps this was a railway station waiting room. Only where? At what station?

But already a rostrum has been set up, from two tables, and some fellow has clambered onto it in a frock coat and with a crooked cravat. From a crumpled piece of paper full of holes, he delivers a speech to the nation. But what speech? He stutters and one can hear only separate words.

Just a moment longer and they will roll onto the stage; through all the doors will run the ragamuffins, women and men, with packages, with bundles, with baskets. Among them will be both the parish priest from Wielopole, with a white cross, and the two twin Hasidim with a large, shapeless oblong bundle, like a rolled-up carpet, which they will not abandon for even a moment. I thought that this was the rolled-up Torah; however, Kantor called it 'the last lifeline'. In this tangle of bodies, tatters and packages, in browns and greys, in the terrifying and trembling ballet of a railway waiting room at the hour of escape, one can recognize—here saved in memory and seemingly restored from a theatrical museum—not only persons and figures from Kantor's former plays but also the props: the old photographic camera, whose extended lens transforms into a machine gun from the First World War; a trough in which there lies a rat-man with a huge bandaged phallus; a coop from which a young woman emerges, in black panties and black bra, clucking like a chicken (perhaps she is Princess Kremlińska from Witkacy's *Dainty Shapes and Hairy Apes,* or else *The Water Hen* construed as a literally embodied metaphor); finally, a gallows rolled in on wheels and, also, on the podium, the mannequin/double of the waiter, standing motionless in the doorway with a napkin draped over his arm. And, in this whole dreamy intermingling of bodies, costumes and objects, we see a pensive Kantor, at moments as if absent; although, this time, this theatre of returning apparitions, which he has invoked, begins to overwhelm him, as if he has ceased to rule it, as if this theatre has absorbed him too. In this carousel of bodies, Kantor for the first time descends from the stage and through the door, which will close after him and open as he returns with a black coffin. He will stroke it like a violin. It will remain beside him almost to the very end.

The charwoman with the spilling bosom will now bring Kantor a torn coat and a wide, crumpled hat. Or, perhaps this is not a charwoman, but one of the characters from *Wielopole*, called by Kantor the returning 'exile from Siberia'. Now, the waiter will be dressed in this exilic coat. Kantor will now push the hat low onto the waiter's forehead and will wrap his face up in a scarf. He will be called Odysseus. And quotes from Wyspiański will resound, as if from far away.

But even a Polish ear and eye are not always able to distinguish apparitions and phantoms of the Polish theatre from Kantor's own apparitions and phantoms. This transformed waiter looks like a scarecrow. And this scarecrow will remain, perhaps to the very end of the show, one of the figures of death.

In Kantor, a theatrical sign/image often has a manifold and not-always-clear symbolic function; but, as in Fellini, it remains beneath the eyelids, knocks about in dreams and is in itself an ikon and a sense, like the figure of Christ hung on cables from a helicopter and rising above Rome or, as in *8½*, a sea monster on a beach at dawn. The stage is suddenly laid waste. Now the twin Hasidim run on, wearing the scarlet cassocks and mitres of cardinals, dancing an Argentine tango. They will disappear, and this same Argentine tango will be danced across the stage by the parish priest from Wielopole, with a raised cross like a female dance partner. And again, for the second time and for the fourth time, the cardinals/Hasidim will dance this dream-like tango with the priest from Wielopole.

I was very tired at this Berlin premier and I think that once, and maybe even twice, I dozed off briefly. But this sleep was not empty. In my dream there returned, mixed with one another, those characters, mannequins and props: the broken legs of the gynecological chair, a cradle and even the dry clack of clappers on the holiday of Purim, from *Wielopole, Wielopole*. And, perhaps it was precisely in this brief dream that I grasped yet another truth. I am afraid to express myself fully. There are moments, sometimes not even very terrible, when the whole of life returns as if in one drop of sleep. These are moments of dark—or, perhaps, actually clear—consciousness before the end. *I will never return here.*

Not long before the end of the performance, the actors and mannequins sit, as if stuck together, on stacked tables and stools, as if on the school benches from *The Dead Class*. The priest summons the dead, in turn, by name and surname. Kantor, for the last time, celebrates his Forefather's Eve. In this assembly of the dead, his father, Marian Kantor, is also present.

The stage empties once more, I think. And yet again, onto the stage will roll: the two Hasidim with their Torah 'life-line', tightly rolled up in paper; the parish priest from Wielopole with a cross; old women with huge bundles on their backs; ladies from the city in torn furs; peddlers with bursting suitcases tied up with twine. Someone shouts something, someone raises his hand towards heaven, to signal that something approaches. But what? But who? But from which direction? Some dates are mentioned: among them, 1945. Yet, this despairing escape, repeated many times, stubbornly and obsessively, contains all escapes to nowhere and all deportations, from the Urals to the Odra.

It is now close to the end. From the lens of that same old-fashioned camera, someone shoots at the crowd as with a machine gun. They sow bullets wide, methodically and systematically, until no one remains alive.

Bodies slump one upon another, until there rises from the corpses, from the suitcases, from the baskets and the 'lifelines', a still life composed of the dead. Now the elegant mourners/gravediggers come on, in top hats and frock coats. They slowly cover this huge pile of corpses in shrouds of black canvas, to the accompaniment of the rising and falling 'Rákóczi March', from the oratorio of Berlioz's *The Damnation of Faust*. In this mass grave, one can also see how, for a moment, the priest's white cross emerges from the shrouds. Yet, a moment later, it again collapses among black sheets. These mourning shrouds contain all the shades of black, as in the huge black canvases of Goya in Madrid's Prado. And Kantor's vision is comparable only to the cruelty of *Caprichos*. But this was still not the end. The charwoman who had run after the army orchestra, on her knees and with a rolled-up skirt, humming the old Hassidic song 'Ani Ma'amin', will now crawl under the shrouds and begin to pull the corpses slowly out from under them, one after another, right until the last. She will drag them behind the wings and the doors will close behind them for the final time. She will remain alone upon the empty stage. She no longer washes the floor. She will climb onto the abandoned rostrum. She opens her lips. She wants to say something. She has no words.

'I will never return here.' When—during the last performance, at the La MaMa theatre in New York—the clapping, which had continued unabated, fell silent at last, the undefeated 'La MaMa', the immortal Ellen Stewart, stepped onto the stage: 'In a year, Kantor will return with *The Dead Class*.'

Stony Brook, July 1988

MEMORY . . . BUT WHAT MEMORY?

The scene is a ruined railway station on the
Odra, two or maybe even four weeks after
the end of military operations. Bohdan
Korzeniewski, one of the most distinguished
people of the theatre in Poland after the war,
was—during the German occupation—a
librarian at the Warsaw University Library.
He reached this railway station, in a regained
Silesia, while on the trail of the rare manu-
scripts and priceless theatrical collections of
the National Library, which had been carried
off by the Germans. He recovered them in
the basements of German counts, packed
them in crates and loaded them onto an
army transport. The Polish 'recovered terri-
tories' were still under Russian occupation.
At night, the future theoretician and practi-
tioner of the theatre returned to the station,
concerned about the recovered treasure.

From the wagons of a long train came strange sounds: rattling, buzzing, at times something akin to cuckooing, at other times to chiming. The wagons had been loaded with plunder; they were full of grandfather clocks, tolling regularly and still in working order. Suddenly, some officer appeared, who was visibly drunk, because he began to shoot a revolver at the windows of the wagons with the tolling clocks.

If he had shot at these bourgeois clocks, tolling the hours with cuckoos or carillons, not with a revolver but with a barrel emerging from an old photographic camera, we would find ourselves unexpectedly in Kantor's theatre. In this real scene—on the platform of a small railway station in Silesia—brooded over by an eyewitness nearly half a century later, we find the incoherence and discontinuity of objects and events, which, it had seemed to us, were revealed only in poetry and in surrealist or post-surrealist painting. A train in which clocks cuckoo might seem like a gripping setting for an as-yet-unwritten work from the theatre of the absurd; however, this 'absurdity', discovered by theatre in the 1950s, first played itself out at this small railway station. *La réalité dépasse la fiction.* On crates containing a priceless book collection taken out of Warsaw, in a Russian train departing for the east, plundered clocks toll romantic carillons. Props become signs. In Kantor's theatre, they become signs of memory. This is history commemorated.

This time the scene is a baroque cathedral in Poznań, in those same first weeks after liberation. The narrator is once again Korzeniewski, the future director of *The Un-Divine Comedy* and *Don Juan.* The vault of the cathedral had been smashed by a bomb; through the huge hole above the central nave swirled flakes of May snow. The blast must have been strong—recounts the narrator—since the baroque figures had fallen from the altars. However, they were scattered about on the floor in some strange positions. If a head had fallen off, the figure now held it in its hands, like a beheaded martyr in a medieval painting. But these were not statues, they were human remains that had been taken from the tombs. They were well preserved, often still with skin stretched on their skulls, stripped of valuables, but bearing the remnants of silk and cloth of gold. Someone must have had their fun with them, since male skeletons had been laid upon the corpses of women with their shin-bones spread wide. In this baroque cathedral, in the scintillating light falling through the coloured fragments of smashed stained-glass windows, profaned corpses had been summoned, as if to enact a renaissance Dance of Death. In this cathedral, smashed by artillery shells, the martyred statues of saints had become doubles of the martyred dead. As in Kantor's theatre, where the dead are the doubles of the living; and the living, doubles of the dead.

In the small Mexican town of Guanajuato, about a thousand miles from the American border, the dead had for decades been buried in a muddy hillside. In this province of incessant poverty, people could not afford coffins. Not many years ago,

FIGURE 6. A sink from *Let the Artists Die*.

after yet another earthquake, mummified remains fell out of the hillside. *La Momia más Pequeña del Mundo* are now placed under glass, in display cabinets. In this Pompeii of Mexican destitution, one can look at naked little corpses of children, with mouths agape as if in permanent astonishment, corpses of women with black stockings clothing legs on which the skin is still stretched, corpses of men with phalluses erect in death. And, perhaps even more harrowing—the heads of men and women, which have fallen off, wearing headbands or scarves, but always with their teeth bared in a grin. Here, death is as obscene as in the Poznań cathedral, with its plundered tombs.

To this day, in carnival processions and celebrations, as once in the Roman Saturnalia, death masks accompany nuptial masks—in Sicily, on the squares of Madrid and Barcelona, in Rio and in the most tumble-down towns and starving villages of Mexico.

In Kantor's theatre, the dead return to take their places on their old school benches. They push aside, and drag beyond the wings,

the doubles of their childhoods. The class
died long ago, the doubles are mannequins.
In *Wielopole, Wielopole*, the recruits in uniforms from the First World War—who
goose-stepped in a parade march—become,
a moment later, mannequins with pasty
faces, thrown into a mass grave. The double
of the bride, still in her veil and white dress,
lies now with legs thrown apart, after being
gang-raped by soldiers. The prelate/uncle
from *Wielopole*, Kantor's family saga, who
married the young couple and blessed the
recruits departing for war, will hang on a
heavy cross, which is rolled onto the stage in
a blasphemous evocation of the mystery of
Christ's Passion. In Kantor's theatre, death is
desecrated and the *sacrum* profaned. In
Book 4 of *Gargantua and Pantagruel*,
Rabelais used the term 'tragic farce' (*cette
tragique farce*)—being perhaps the first to
coin it—to name the profanation of the
Easter mystery by Master Francois Villon
(*Maître François Villon*).Villon had ordered
boys dressed up as devils to scare, almost to
death, a sacristan who had refused to lend

his liturgical vestments to a peasant chosen to depict God the Father in the mystery play. An unsaddled mare dragged off the poor sacristan, in this devilry improvised by Villon.

In the tragi-farce of Kantor, as in the tragi-farce of Beckett—since, in the end, and despite the entire dissimilarity of their imagery, how to avoid comparing these two theatres of the end of our century?—birthing is dying. In *Dead Class,* one gives birth on a broken dentist's chair, in *Endgame* one dies in a rubbish bin. Birth and death are degraded; but, in both of these theatres, they remain an unyielding and incessant memory.

Kantor—who is present to the end, during all of his theatrical performances, urging his actors on with an impatient shaking of the fingers—I have compared to Charon, who conveys the dead to the other side of the Lethe of Oblivion. But Kantor is a Charon who conveys the dead back to our side, across the River of Memory. And it is perhaps for this reason that this once-silent Greek Charon now always shouts so terribly, at both the dead/living and the living/dead. He conveys them, if only for an hour, if only as their own doubles/mannequins. In Polish folk tradition, the cemetery is called 'the park of stiffs'.

Kantor/Charon, in his black clothes and felt hat, *is* memory, the memory of childhood and familial memory; the memory of a room that *was*, built on the stage from a few of small wooden boards ('only we were absent from this room'); and even the memory of the forgotten clatter of the clappers which boys, in the real Wielopole, struck on Good Friday. In this theatre of obsessive memory there appear: school benches, faded family photos and—during the roll-call of the dead in *I Shall Never Return*—the name and surname of Kantor's father, Marian Kantor.

One must be deaf, in order not to hear, in the work of Kantor, this theme of biography-as-graveyard. There is a shadow in this theatre—I am unable properly to name it—a shadow of a world that was, once and for all, erased and which only occasionally returns, stubbornly summoned by some compulsion of memory; hence those melodies, which fade and return, now almost deafening, as in that Viennese waltz in *The Dead Class*, or— now in other registers of painful, tender melody—the Jewish lullabies and songs of Hasidim.

In this theatre of memory, of Charon the ferryman, in every performance right until the last, all of his theatres perpetually return, starting from the first, Cricot, with its mannequins of men and women with uncovered genitals, and its coop in which a whore is a hen. The famous urinal of Duchamp is now forever an *objet d'art*. But, in Kantor, a dentist's chair on which a birth occurs, or a washbasin into which a charwoman wrings dirty water from a rag, are never *objets d'art*. They are, perhaps, also a provocation, but never a provocation meant for aesthetes. In this lies Kantor's otherness.

In this sudden mixing of cages for human fowl, of broken cradles, of gallows rolled on stage and carpets rolled up like holy Torahs, in this sudden proximity—as at that railway station at the end of the war—of stolen and cuckooing clocks and plundered rarities from the libraries of Warsaw, is played out the common, mortal human comedy. In this so-very-Polish theatre, in which echo-images, echo-symbols, echo-quotes—from Mickiewicz and Witkiewicz, Wyspiański and Gombrowicz—tangle together and so strangely bond, Kantor's new, mortal human comedy is universal.

Kantor's is a travelling theatre, perhaps the only one remaining in our times. And precisely in this, it is at once and unexpectedly akin to the Elizabethan theatre, whose actors travelled for months on the shores of the Baltic and through the Hanseatic cities, and which, even in Shakespeare's life, brought three of his works to cities from Königsberg to Krakow, transporting their rich costumes, their weapons—and even a cage with the head of an executed rebel—on huge wagons harnessed to Percherons. And, in this wandering, Kantor's theatre is also similar to Moliere's first company, which, travelling from palaces to inns, transported on its wagons the costumes of fools, theatrical scripts at times still handwritten, along with the white powders and rouges for the actors. They also carried a cradle, because— as with Kantor's troupe—Moliere's first theatre was like a large family. I can easily imagine Kantor's theatre travelling on a wagon from Krakow to Paris.

I saw Kantor's performances in Nancy, in Florence, in Berlin and in New York's La MaMa. I even met some devoted viewers of this theatre, who wandered after Kantor like ducks after a wagon or, rather, like seagulls after a ship. Clearly, this theatre provides some nourishment, even if bitter, though it is different from the wide world's other shows. Perhaps it is like this also because Kantor— like only a few artists of our time—has translated into theatrical signs a forgotten memory, which is present in every one of us like a badly healed wound. And perhaps in this, precisely, lies the cathartic role of Kantor/Charon, who restores the dead.

Santa Monica, May 1989

TADEUSZ KANTOR, 1915–1990

It was still so recently that I wrote about him—present always on the stage, in his black clothes, trousers with suspenders and a soft felt hat—how with a light movement of his hands, like a flick of the fingers, he ferried his actors like Charon across the Styx to the realm of oblivion, in order that they return in memory. He transformed the living into the dead, then changed the dead in turn into the living. Now he has passed away and has himself become only a memory.

He was one of the greatest, most consistent and most stubborn innovators of contemporary theatre. No one, to whom it was given to watch the theatre of Kantor, will ever forget his mannequins as actors and actors as mannequins, the hallucinatory return of musical refrains, the houses and rooms—which had long ago ceased to exist—created, out of a few boards, on an empty stage. But the greatness of Kantor lies in more than the renewal of a dead art.

I have watched his performances in New York's La MaMa, in Paris, in Berlin; each time, it seemed to me that I saw the same audience. In contrast with specious innovation and the illusions of form, Kantor's theatre restored a shared and universal memory: the memory of war, the memory of cruelty, the memory of the dead.

His was, perhaps, one of the last travelling theatres: from Krakow to New York, from Florence to Tokyo, from Europe to both Americas and to Asia. In each of these places, he restored to viewers, in his own language—which became their common tongue—their own forgotten memory and that of their fathers. He called his theatre a place of death. But only a year ago, in Paris, he spoke of his art as a theatre of death and love. He called his last show *I Shall Never Return*. But Kantor—tireless to the very end, reviling death, of which he was perpetually aware—was already cooking up a new performance, to which he gave the title *Today Is My Birthday*.

The last Polish Charon of contemporary world theatre is now and will remain only a memory. But this memory contains not only death but also birth. A birth is a negation of death. Memory is always a birth. A restoration of the dead to the living.

Santa Monica, December 1990

Kantor died a short time before my fifth heart attack. He was taken away during his last rehearsal. In the hospital, he did not regain consciousness. He died before dawn. From the perspective of death everything becomes a sign. As in Shakespeare's *The Tempest*, which is both tragedy and comedy, in which it sometimes seems to us we hear his voice. As in Kantor's *Today Is My Birthday* and *I Shall Never Return*. I saw him for the last time in Paris. It was his festival and one of his greatest triumphs: exhibitions, all of his plays performed in halls full to the brim. Finally, a three-day symposium, in the Centre Pompidou, from morning till late afternoon, also in a packed hall, with speeches by experts and celebrities, interrupted constantly by Kantor's shouts.

He shouted at all the speakers. As he did during rehearsals, at technicians and actors. He shouted terribly. Everything was always not quite right: too early, too late, misplaced. At these debates in the Centre Pompidou, as each evening on the stage, he was again the greatest actor. As he also was in Krakow, even when he walked across the Mariacki Square. He was himself his own incomparable theatre. I wrote of him that, like Charon, he ferries the dead, but restores what is forgotten. Even when the dead return as mannequins. Charon also returned. But Kantor, who restored the dead to the living, will not now himself return. He consumed himself in his intransigent demand for the ultimate Kantor. Until he burnt out.

Santa Monica, January 1991

POST-MORTEM

An empty chair. This is the title I wanted
to give this note, but Bronisław Mamoń
pre-empted me, with a penetrating discus-
sion of *Today Is My birthday*, in *Tygodnik*
Powszechny. An empty chair. I imagined that
it would stand on the stage-platform, from
the first lights till the end of the performance. This chair stood on the left side of the
platform; upon it, once again, sat Kantor. He
wore that soft hat of his and a black woollen
scarf thrown over his shoulder. He had his
face turned three-quarters towards the
wings. As if living. In this theatre, in which
actors and their likenesses replace one
another in turn, I thought that he was the
mannequin of Kantor. But this mannequin
rose from the chair, began to walk and even
repeated, with Kantor's gesture, that impatient flick of the fingers. From a tape came

Kantor's voice—then, only the voice of an intruder.

I understand Kantor's primordial intention/invention and the attempt to maintain it, made by those who would continue his work. In this 'poor room of the imagination', a changing/unchanging frame of evocation is provided by three empty stretchers of different sizes, moved across the stage in turn. Figures enter into them and exit out of them and, in them, are doubled. Kantor wanted this 'birthday' ritual to serve as his 'self-portrait'. Just as he lent his father a twin, who 'took his face'. Just as the Infanta from Velázquez, in crinoline stretched on metal scaffolding, is displaced, indeed many times, by a 'poor girl, who is not there'. The crinoline is cut open and when one parts its tails, one can see her sex barely concealed by underwear. And similarly, when she is brought a skirt, the 'indigent girl', the poor double of the Infanta, shows her threadbare panties.

The double was to be a replica of Kantor, but a replica of his presence. When Kantor was no longer there, the 'self-portrait' became a caricature. Poor Kantor is in a painter's studio—and this is probably the guiding principle of this last evocation—models enter and step down from picture frames. But in this 'poor room' of imprisoned imagination, this poor room with a bucket for laundering dirty washing and still the same little iron stove, the history of a family is summoned: a history Polish but not only Polish, both personal and common, in which Maria Jarema and Meyerhold, martyred by Stalinist thugs, Jews pushed into pits and raped women all exist together. Everything in this one and always the same room of his memory.

In this poor room of memory, there is also a small table with an old photograph, salvaged from the past it seems, since it is very damaged. As are also the photographs of my parents. His father, mother, dear uncle Stasio and the prelate from Wielopole stand now as if living—in the largest of the frames, in the depths of the stage—and lift up in a birthday toast their small shot glasses, with the same mechanical motion as in the films of the 1920s. The double lifts the photo, looks at his father in the frame and shouts: 'Daddy!' But even more poignant is the scene—it sends shivers down the spine— when the twins bring in a board like a coffin. At the funeral, Wacław and Lesław Janicki carried Kantor's coffin to the grave in just this way.

After the New York performance of *Today Is My Birthday*, I drank vile wine in a small restaurant on the same street as La MaMa. I was with friends, all of them one or two generations younger than me. We were not cheerful. We felt as if after a wake. We were—here my electric typewriter, writing too fast and in my stead, suggests a word which I would rather not write—*umęczeni*. This word contains both 'exhaustion' and 'martyrdom'. The youngest of us, Magda, spoke first: 'Why does he exhaust us like this? Why does he do it again, just as he did before? I don't want these nightmares any longer.' I answered that it is in the nature of nightmares that they return. We wake with a shout, our wife calms us, we fall asleep and wake again with the same shout. The nightmare has returned. I said that the greatest creators were prisoners of their own nightmares: like Goya and Fuseli, or like Lebenstein, who was even closer to Kantor. And like Fellini—perhaps the closest to Kantor, though I think no one recalled him—who discovered in the circus the essence of life, which dwells next door to death. All of them lived and died, or die and live, choked by their own nightmare.

Kantor was the one most faithful to his nightmares. In the performance, *Today Is My Birthday,* the packaging from early Cricot returns. *Emballage. Emballage . . . between eternity and garbage.* Only that now it returns not in the form of paper bags but of nylon sacks. From the first scene, bodies in packaging are scattered across the stage. In this Kantorian ritual, they will then enter an empty frame, coming to life and dying. From these frames will tumble, like a vast symphony *en blanc majeur*, a procession of crippled women in hospital robes, in a

distant echo of Brecht's *Threepenny Opera*.
These bodies, unpacked, will then be raped
and killed once more, to return again in the
final funeral march, bearing white crosses.
At a certain moment, during each performance of Kantor's work, I close my eyes and
enter into my own terrors.

In the theatre, vibrations pass not only
between the stage and the audience, but also
between the audience and what is beyond
the stage. In the performance on East Fourth
Street, in New York, I think that not only the
actors but almost all of the audience were
from Poland. Poland was close. The spectacle
was still disturbing, but differently, I think,
from in the past. Poland's martyrology, and
everything from the First World War to the
Jaruzelskian, grew dim. It was as if everything were covered in mould and fog. We
received *Today Is My Birthday* with bitter-
ness in our throats.

How much longer can this theatre last?
Months? A year and a few months? Theatres
live briefly. Sometimes even more briefly
than their creators. And perhaps the happiest

outcome is when they die together with their creators. Kantor's actors lived by this theatre. This theatre was their life. I understand that they cannot part with it. Not only from piety towards Kantor, but also for themselves, they want to extend its duration. I do not want to be cruel, but without Kantor this theatre is like a body without a soul. Kantor gave a soul even to packaging and mannequins. Kantor's theatre dwells on this brittle and fleeting border between what still endures and what has already become memory.

The memory of theatre is brittle. It endures beneath the eyelids of its last spectators. And I understand the concern that there should remain as many of these as possible. But what endures beneath the eyelids of spectators who cannot now watch this theatre *with* Kantor should not be a body without a soul. The example of the Berliner Ensemble is telling and serves as a warning. A theatre is not a place for its own museum. In place of the image of Kantor, the living Kantor—from his inimitable flick of the fingers to his terrible shout—I would not want there to arise in memory even the most well-crafted double.

Various and distinct are the ways the greats of theatre linger in the memory: in the eye, in the ear, sometimes even in things. When, almost a year ago, I was helped with difficulty up the steep stairs to the hall on the highest floor of the Warsaw theatre school, which had once housed the Piarist Collegium Nobilium and then the rituals of the Masons, and where I was now to speak about contemporary drama, I heard the rap of Zelwerowicz's cane and the muffled laugh of Schiller.

In the Comédie-Française, they preserve Molière's armchair like a relic or a treasure. I do not recall if it is upholstered in leather, or in a now-largely-decayed cloth of gold, from beneath which horse hair springs. After Molière, no one ever sat in this armchair. No one dared. After Kantor, may only an empty chair remain.

Stony Brook, July 1991

FIGURE 7. A bed, the workshop of death,
from *Wielopole, Wielopole*.

A MEMORY APART

In the five years since Kantor's passing, his theatre of death has already become, once and for all and ultimately, a theatre of memory: his memory, our memory—we who have retained his form, wearing a black felt hat, the gesture of the fingers by which he summoned and dismissed the dead—and that memory apart, the most enduring, imprisoned in things. In this postmortem memory, all times mingle in the lowest of beings. Because memory, though almost always brittler than things, has also its own time apart, in which all memories are mixed at once.

I realized this two, perhaps, or maybe even three years ago, at a Krakow exhibition in the National Museum. I wandered there among props from four performances, including among these some from *The Water*

Hen, from before *The Dead Class*. There were school benches and the old-fashioned camera, which transformed into a machine gun from the First World War; also, that room without walls, from *Wielopole* I think, in which certain uncles lived, and where two twins now searched for old windows; and, I think in the last of the exhibitions, again that 'poor room of the imagination', in which Maria Jarema briefly lived and which was haunted suddenly by Meyerhold, murdered in the Lubyanka. It was in this poor room, if I remember right, that Velázquez's Infanta appeared; and, even earlier, it was, after all, from this room that The Charwoman/Death exited, she whose ample bosom spilt out of her apron when she washed the floor. This 'poor room of the imagination' became many rooms of memory, in the Museum of the Cricot Theatre and in the Krakow Gallery on Sienna Street.

And maybe now more clearly than in Kantor's lifetime—but after all, this ferryman across the Styx of oblivion himself never knew death—we see how poor were so many avant-gardes, local and foreign, in comparison with this theatre of the dead. For in this junk room, which is already a museum, the inconsistent memory of spectators has been preserved—both us, here, and all the others scattered on the paths of this itinerant theatre, across two hemispheres and three continents. Once more, in this 'poor theatre', a common memory is brought to light. And this is why Kantor still remains among us.

Santa Monica, All Souls, 1995

AUTHOR'S AFTERWORD

The year was 1971 or 1972. I was
by the sea, in a small town, almost a
village. There was a single street of
small, poor, single-storey houses,
one of which, perhaps the poorest,
was a school. It was summer, during
the holidays. The school was empty
and abandoned. It had only one
classroom. It was possible to observe
it through the dusty panes of two
small, wretched windows, set low
just above the pavement. This gave
the impression that the school had
sunk below the level of the street. I
stuck my face to the panes. For a
very long time I stood peeking into
the dark and cloudy depths of my
memory.

Thus begins the first of five pages of notes, written by Tadeusz Kantor in 1982. This note is not only a personal confession gripping in its simplicity. It is, equally, a record of the moment at which the theatre of memory was born.

> I was a small boy again. I sat in a poor village classroom, on a bench wounded by penknives, moistening the pages of a primer with fingers stained by ink. The grain of the floorboards had been worn right back from constant scrubbing and the bare feet of village boys were somehow in harmony with this floor. Whitewashed walls, plaster falling off them at the bottom. On one wall, a black cross.

He also mentions seeing, in an astonishing illumination, his own theatre of memory, which had not yet arisen:

> Today I know that there, by that window, something important occurred. I made a certain discovery.

> Somehow, with an uncommon
> starkness, I became aware of *the
> existence of memory.*

In the pages of this small book, I have written several times of Kantor/Charon, as of one who summons the dead. But I failed to write that it is not only the dead. This new Charon summons not only dead people. Kantor also summons dead things. He restores to memory its visibility. In *The Dead Class* there return not only the doubles of the dead; what is visible, indeed most visible, are the school benches, or, rather, their doubles.

Much has been written about the physical presence of Kantor, sitting always on the same chair, at every one of his shows. But, as far as I know, no one has asked why this was the case. Kantor, like Waki—who, in the ritual theatre of Noh, rarely leaves his chair—or like a hypnotist, of both his actors and his audience, restores visibility to those school benches, which he once saw through a dusty window pane. These are those benches, those rooms, those old photographs, restored to memory. For a moment regained, in order to depart, again, into oblivion—beyond the wings.

EMBALLAGE . . .
EMBALLAGE . . .

This is still from the Cricot 2 manifesto of February 1964.

When
one wants to shelter something
safeguard it
that it endure,
to fix,
to flee before time—
EMBALLAGE . . .
When
one wants to hide something deep
EMBALLAGE . . .

In this fixing of memory, in the summoning of it as something visible, Kantor made use of objects taken from a *reality* of, as he put it, 'the lowest rank'. Not only the wheel, as in Marcel Duchamp, but a sink, a rat trap, a bath, a suitcase, a gynecologist's chair, a cradle and a hen coop. But, as with the students' doubles in *The Dead Class,* these are the doubles of objects from Kantor's workshop.

And now, one last quote from this record of seeing, of 1971 or 1972:

> The window awakens dread and a sense of that which is 'beyond'. And the absence of children gives the impression that those children have already lived out their lives, that they have died, and that it is only through this fact of their *having died*— through death—that this classroom becomes filled with recollections, and that only then do these recollections start to live. . . .

The theatre of memory was a theatre of death.

Kaddish—this is the title I gave to these *Pages on Tadeusz Kantor*. Photographs of performances can be a valuable form of documentation but always seem to me like something dead. In this modest book, we decided to include as illustrations some preserved family photographs and reproductions of objects from Kantor's workshop, which were the substance of his vision and the raw material of his theatre.

The initiator and co-author of this book is Piotr Kłoczwoski, who chose the illustrations and from the start surrounded its publication with his care. In both his name and my own, I wish to thank Maria Kantor and Lech Stangret for their help in choosing photographs and for granting us permission to use them. We also thank the Krakow Cricoteka for their assistance.

Santa Monica, January 1997

FIGURE 8. A wardrobe from *Wielopole, Wielopole*—
that important interior of the imagination

EDITOR'S NOTES

The essays and fragments collected here, corrected and completed, first appeared in the following publications:

'He Spoke a Throaty French . . .', as 'Italian Journals' (fragment), in *Aloes: Journals and Short Sketches*, Warsaw, 1966.

'Essences' is the first part of a paper delivered at an international symposium in Novi Sad, Serbia, in May, 1982. The whole text, 'The Theatre of Essence: Kantor and Brook', was published in *Zeszyty Literackie,* no. 2, Paris, 1983.

'In Mickiewicz', as 'ŻmutWhat Kind of Form is This?' (fragment), in *Zeszyty Literackie*, no. 20, Paris, 1987. In the text, I quote a fragment of Jarosław Marek Rymkiewicz's book *Żmut* (Paris: Sic!, 1987).

'At What Station?', as 'Kantor's Kaddish', in *Zeszyty Literackie,* no. 24, Paris, 1988.

'Memory . . . But What Kind of Memory?', in Zeszyty Literackie, no. 27, Paris, 1989. In this text, I recall an incident described by Małgorzata Szejnert in the book *Fame and Infamy: Conversations with Bohdan Korzeniewski* (London: Aneks, 1988).

The first part of 'Tadeusz Kantor 1915–1990' was published in *Polish Review*, New York, 13 December 1990; the second part, 'My Fifth Heart Attack' (fragment), in *Zeszyty Literackie*, no. 34, Paris, 1991.

'Post-Mortem', as 'Kantor: Post Mortem', in *Polish Review*, New York, 11 December 1991.

'A Memory Apart', as 'Two Pages: A Memory Apart', in *Polish Review*, New York, 17 December 1995.

ROK 1971 LUB 72 .   NAD MORZEM . W MAŁEJ MIEŚCINIE.
PRAWIE WIEŚ .   JEDNA ULICA . MAŁE BIEDNE PARTERO=
WE DOMKI . I JEDEN CHYBA NAJBIEDNIEJSZY : SZKOŁA .
BYŁO LATO I WAKACJE .   SZKOŁA BYŁA PUSTA I OPUSZ=
CZONA . MIAŁA TYLKO JEDNĄ KLASĘ . MOŻNA JĄ BYŁO OGLĄ=
DAĆ PRZEZ ZAKURZONE SZYBY DWU MAŁYCH NĘDZNYCH OKIEN,
UMIESZCZONYCH NISKO TUŻ NAD TROTUAREM .   ROBIŁO TO
WRAŻENIE, ŻE SZKOŁA SIĘ ZAPADŁA PONIŻEJ POZIOMU ULICY.
PRZYLEPIŁEM TWARZ DO SZYB . BARDZO DŁUGO ZAGLĄDAŁEM W
GŁĄB CIEMNĄ I ZMĄCONĄ MOJEJ PAMIĘCI .

BYŁEM ZNOWU MAŁYM CHŁOPCEM , SIEDZIAŁEM W BIEDNEJ WIEJ=
SKIEJ KLASIE , W ŁAWCE POKALECZONEJ KOZIKAMI, POPLAMIONYMI
ATRAMENTEM PALCAMI ŚLINIĄC KARTKI ELEMENTARZA , DESKI
PODŁOGI MIAŁY OD CIĄGŁEGO SZOROWANIA GŁĘBOKO WYTARTE SŁOJE ,
BOSE NOGI WIEJSKICH CHŁOPAKÓW JAKOŚ Z TĄ PODŁOGĄ DOBRZE
KORESPONDOWAŁY .   BIELONE ŚCIANY , TYNK ODPADAJĄCY DOŁEM ,
NA ŚCIANIE CZARNY KRZYŻ.

DZIŚ WIEM, ŻE TAM PRZY TYM O K N I E   STAŁO SIĘ COŚ
WAŻNEGO .   DOKONAŁEM PEWNEGO ODKRYCIA . JAKOŚ NIEZWYK=
LE JASKRAWO UZMYSŁOWIŁEM SOBIE
I S T N I E N I E
W S P O M N I E N I A .

TO STWIERDZENIE WCALE NIE JEST , JAKBY SIĘ MOGŁO TO WYDAĆ ,
WYNIKIEM EGZALTACJI I PRZESADY .
WSPOMNIENIE W NASZYM RACJONALNYM ŚWIECIE NIE MIAŁO NAJ=
LEPSZEJ SŁAWY I NIE LICZYŁO SIĘ KOMPLETNIE W ZIMNYCH
ROZRACHUNKACH Z RZECZYWISTOŚCIĄ .
NAGLE ODKRYŁEM JEGO TAJEMNICZĄ , NIEWYOBRAŻALNA SIŁĘ ,
ODKRYŁEM, ŻE JEST ŻYWIOŁEM, KTÓRY POTRAFI NISZCZYĆ I TWORZYĆ,
ŻE STOI U POCZĄTKU KREACJI , STWORZENIA .
U POCZĄTKU SZTUKI .
WSZYSTKO NAGLE STAŁO SIĘ JASNE , JAKBY OTWARŁY SIĘ LICZNE
DRZWI NA DALEKIE , NIESKOŃCZONE PRZESTRZENIE I PEJZAŻE.

TO JUŻ NIE BYŁ TEN WSTYDLIWY OBJAW LIRYCZNY I SENTYMENTAL=
NY., PRZYPISYWANY STAROŚCI I NIELETNIM PANIENKOM.
JAWIŁ SIĘ W SWOJEJ PRZERAŹLIWEJ, GINĄCEJ RAZ NA ZAWSZE
PERSPEKTYWIE , W BÓLU PRZEMIJANIA I W SŁODYCZY ,
KTÓRĄ RODZI TĘSKNOTA .

POJAWIŁO SIĘ ZROZUMIENIE WIELU RZECZY.
    WSPOMNIENIE   ŻYJE NA RÓWNEJ
STOPIE Z REALNYMI WYDARZENIAMI NASZEGO CODZIENNEGO ŻYCIA .
WCALE NIE STRONI OD NICH , NAWET WRĘCZ PRZECIWNIE , SĄ
MU ONE POTRZEBNE , W JEGO STRATEGICZNYCH PLANACH
I POCIĄGNIĘCIACH,
NA TEJ, NIEUJAWNIONEJ NA MAPIE DNIA CODZIENNEGO , DRODZE
C O F A N I A   S I Ę , KTÓRE GENIALNIE MASKUJE
PRZYGOTOWUJĄCY SIĘ   A T A K
N I E   D O   O D P A R C I A .

I JESZCZE JEDNO ODKRYCIE I ZROZUMIENIE :
WSPOMNIENIE KWESTIONUJE
K O M P E T E N C J E
W I Z U A L N O Ś C I ,
PODAJE W GRUBĄ WĄTPLIWOŚĆ JEJ UZURPATORSKĄ WŁADZĘ .
TEN FAKT,
W TYM CZASIE, GDY STAŁEM PRZED WSPOMNIANYM OKNEM ,
NIE BYŁBY DLA WSPOMNIENIA JAKIMŚ WYJĄTKOWYM POWODEM
CHWAŁY ,   BYŁ TO BOWIEM CZAS, GDY CAŁA SZTUKA TRACIŁA
SZYBKO I POŚPIESZNIE , W SPOSÓB LEKKOMYŚLNY
ZAUFANIE DO W I D Z I A L N O Ś C I .
NATOMIAST UMIESZCZANIE TEGO AKTU NIEUFNOŚCI W ZJAWISKU
TAK , OŚMIELĘ SIĘ RZEC , POGARDZANYM , POSĄDZONYM
O MISTYCYZM I BANALNY LUB STARCZY SENTYMENTALIZM ,
BYŁO
A K T E M   W I E L K I G O   O D S T Ę P S T W A ,
M O I C H   U M I Ł O W A N Y C H   P R A K T Y K ,
RYZYKUJĄCYCH PŁOMIENIE S T O S U   I WYROKI
Ś W I Ę T E J   I N K W I Z Y C J I   R O Z U M U .

WSPOMNIENIE ŻYJE POZA ZASIĘGIEM NASZEGO WZROKU ,
RODZI SIĘ , ROZRASTA W REJONACH NASZEGO UCZUCIA
I WZRUSZENIA .
I PŁACZU .
NIE MOŻNA BYŁO GORZEJ WYBRAĆ , W CZASACH , GDY NIEPODZIELNE
RZĄDY SPRAWOWAŁ TRYBUNAŁ ROZUMU .
BYŁO SIĘ POSĄDZONYM NIE TYLKO O ODSTĘPSTWO ALE
I O ZACOFANIE .
TRZEBA BYŁO MIEĆ MOCNY CHARAKTER   HERETYCKI.
CZUŁEM SIĘ WTEDY WIELKIM HEREZJARCHĄ .

TA NOSTALGJA , KTÓRA JUŻ OD PEWNEGO CZASU CORAZ SILNIEJ
DAWAŁA O SOBIE ZNAĆ ,
TO O L Ś N I E N I E ;
CZYMŚ , CO STAŁO ZA PROGIEM
W I D Z I A L N E G O ,
TAJEMNICZE I IMPERATYWNE ,
TO ODIMYCIE W S P O M N I E N I A
PRZYSZŁO W SAMĄ PORĘ , BO W TEJ WIELKIEJ BATALJI PRZECIW
W I D Z I A L N E M U
I M A T E R I A L N E M U ,
W KTÓREJ ZRESZTĄ SAM BRAŁEM UDZIAŁ ,
WYTOCZONO WŁASNIE NAJCIĘŻSZE DZIAŁA
S C J E N T Y Z M U -
BYŁ MI ON NIESKONCZENIE OBCY !

I ABY ZAMKNĄĆ TEN ROZDZIAŁ
NALEŻAŁO PRZEPROWADZIĆ
R E W I Z J Ę
I R E H A B I L I T A C J Ę   POJĘCIA

P R Z E S Z Ł O Ś C I .
ZROBIŁEM TO .
PROKLAMOWAŁEM WĘDRUJĄC PO ŚWIECIE
T R I U M F
P R Z E S Z Ł O S C I ,
OŚMIELAJĄC SIĘ WIERZYC , ŻE JEST TO JEDYNY CZAS
REALNY I LICZĄCY SIĘ
(W SZTUCE) ,
BO JUŻ DOKONANY !

WKOŃCU NADESZŁA TA PAMIĘTNA DLA MNIE CHWILA
DECYZJI , ŻE NALEŻY
W S P O M N I E N I E   W Y R A Z I Ć .
STAŁO SIĘ WTEDY KONIECZNYM POZNANIE
FUNKCJONOWANIA
P A M I Ę C I .

TAK ROZPOCZĘŁA SIĘ DZIESIĘCIOLETNIA ERA
MOICH DWÓCH DZIEŁ
" UMARŁA KLASA "   I
" WIELOPOLE WIELOPOLE " ,
KTÓRE MIAŁY POTWIERDZIĆ
PRAWDĘ MOICH GŁOSZONYCH BLUŻNIERCZYCH IDEI .
BYŁA TO ERA MOJEJ WŁASNEJ AWANGARDY .
AWANGARDY :
WSPOMNIENIA ,
PAMIĘCI ,
NIEWIDZIALNEGO ,
PUSTKI   I   ŚMIERCI .

ŚMIERĆ .
NA NIEJ KOŃCZY SIĘ TO NIEWINNE POCZĄTKOWO
ZAGLĄDANIE PRZEZ OKNO .
BO OKNO KRYJE WIELE MROCZNYCH TAJEMNIC .
OKNO BUDZI LĘK I PRZECZUCIE TEGO, CO JEST " POZA " .
I TA NIEOBECNOŚĆ DZIECI ,
WRAŻENIE ŻE DZIECI PRZEŻYŁY JUŻ SWOJE ŻYCIE , POMARŁY
I ŻE DOPIERO PRZEZ TEN FAKT P O M A R C I A,
PRZEZ ŚMIERĆ
TA KLASA NAPEŁNIA SIĘ WSPOMNIENIAMI,
I ŻE DOPIERO WTEDY WSPOMNIENIA ZACZYNAJĄ ŻYĆ
I NABIERAJĄ TAJEMNICZEJ MOCY DUCHOWEJ.
NIC NIE JEST OD NICH WTEDY WIĘKSZE , NIC SILNIEJSZE ....

OSTATNIO PO BLISKO 10 LATACH W CIĄGU KTÓRYCH
" UMARŁA KLASA " OBJECHAŁA CAŁY ŚWIAT
UŚWIADOMIŁEM SOBIE JESZCZE JEDEN ASPEKT TEJ FASCYNACJI
" PRZEZ O K N O ".
WIZUALNOŚĆ
JAKO WARUNEK PERCEPCJI ,
TO OGLĄDANIE " OD ZEWNĄTRZ "
TA ZAROZUMIAŁA " DOTYKALNOŚĆ " MATERIALNĄ,
PEDANTERYJNA SPRAWDZALNOŚĆ
WYWOŁAŁY WE MNIE OKREŚLONY SPRZECIW
I DĄŻENIE , BY PRZEKROCZYĆ
P R Ó G   W I D Z I A L N O Ś C I,
TEGO APODYKTYCZNEGO I BEZWZGLĘDNEGO WARUNKU,
TEGO " KABLA " , " PRZEWODU "
JAKOBY JEDYNEGO MOGĄCEGO ZAPEWNIĆ
" O G L Ą D ".

IDEA " UMARŁEJ KLASY " MIAŁA POCZĄTEK WŁAŚNIE
W TYM UŁAMKOWYM , WSTYDLIWYM W I D Z E N I U.
CAŁA METODA SPEKTAKLU FUNKCJONOWAŁA NA ZASADZIE
OGLĄDANIA (CZY TO JEST WOGÓLE " OGLĄDANIE " ?)
TEGO, CO JEST ZASŁONIĘTE SZCZELNIE
NIEPRZENIKLIWĄ SKORUPĄ.

6.

OWĄ OSŁAWIONĄ FORMĄ,
KTÓRA OD TYSIĄCLECI ROŚCI SOBIE PRETENSJE
DO BYCIA TREŚCIĄ I ISTOTĄ DZIEŁA .
JEST NAJWĘŻSZYM NIETAKTEM
NIE CHCIEĆ POPRZESTAĆ NA TYM " Z E W N Ą T R Z " .
USIŁOWAĆ OBRAŹLIWIE JE OBEJŚĆ
PRÓBOWAĆ OGLĄDNĄĆ INACZEJ,
OD " W E W N Ą T R Z ",
PODGLĄDNĄĆ .

NIE JEST TO TAKIE ŁATWE .
CENA, KTÓRĄ SIĘ ZA TO PŁACI JEST
S P O T K A N I E   Z E   Ś M I E R C I Ą .

KANTOR'S TYPESCRIPT

The year was 1971 or 1972. I was by the sea,
in a small town, almost a village. There was a
single street of small, poor, single-story
houses, one of which, perhaps the poorest,
was a school. It was summer, during the holidays. The school was empty and abandoned.
It had only one classroom. It was possible to
observe it through the dusty panes of two
small, wretched windows, set low just above
the pavement. This gave the impression that
the school had sunk below the level of the
street. I stuck my face to the panes. For a
very long time I stood peeking into the dark
and cloudy depths of my memory.

I was a small boy again. I sat in a poor
village classroom, on a bench wounded by
penknives, moistening the pages of a primer
with fingers stained by ink. The grain of the
floorboards had been worn right back from

constant scrubbing and the bare feet of village boys were somehow in harmony with this floor. Whitewashed walls, plaster falling off them at the bottom. On one wall, a black cross.

Today I know that there, by that window, something important occurred. I made a certain discovery. Somehow, with an uncommon starkness, I became aware of *the existence of memory.* This statement is not, as it might seem to be, a result of exaltation or exaggeration. In our rational world, memory did not have the best reputation and did not count at all in cold reckonings with reality. Suddenly, I discovered its mysterious, unimaginable power. I discovered that it is an element that is able to destroy and to create, that it stands at the origins of creation, of the created world, of art. Everything suddenly became clear, as if numerous doors had opened upon distant, unending spaces and landscapes.

This was no longer that shameful, lyrical and sentimental display ascribed to old age and to immature girls. It appeared in its dreadful aspect, vanishing once and for all, in the pain of transience and in the sweetness which gives birth to longing.

An understanding of many things emerged. Memory dwells at the same level as the real events of our ordinary life. It does not shun them at all; even quite the opposite, they are necessary for it, for its strategic plans and moves on that path of retreat— unrevealed on the map of the everyday— which brilliantly masks the irresistible attack that is preparing itself.

There was one other discovery and understanding: memory brings into question the competence of visuality. It brings into serious doubt its usurpatory power. At the time when I stood before the window I have mentioned, this fact would not have been, for memory, some exceptional cause for praise, since this was a time when art as a whole was swiftly and hurriedly, and in a reckless manner, losing its trust in visibility. However, locating this act of mistrust in a phenomenon so, I dare say, scorned, suspected of mysticism and a banal or senile sentimentality, was an act of great apostasy on the part of my beloved practices, which thus risked the flames of the pyre and the verdicts of reason's holy inquisition.

Memory lives beyond the reach of our gaze; it is born and grows in regions of our feelings and affections. And tears could not have been a worse choice, during times when the tribunal of reason exercised absolute control. One was suspected not only of apostasy but also of regression. It was necessary to have a strong, heretical character. At that time, I felt myself to be a great heresiarch.

This nostalgia, which from a certain moment made itself known ever more strongly, this enlightenment by something standing beyond the threshold of the visible, mysterious and imperative, this discovery of memory, all came at just the right time, because in that great campaign against the visible and material—in which I, in any case, took part—the heaviest ordnance was rolled out against scientism, which was endlessly foreign to me.

And, in order to close this chapter, it was necessary to carry out a rehabilitation of the concept of the past. I did this. Wandering across the world, I proclaimed the triumph of the past, daring to believe that it is the only time that is both real and of account in art, since it is already accomplished.

At last there arrived a moment memorable to me—the decision that memory must be articulated. It then became necessary to get to know the functioning of memory.

Thus began the decade-long era of my two works, *Dead Class* and *Wielopole, Wielopole*, which were to confirm the truth of the blasphemous ideas I had proclaimed. This was the era of my own avant-garde: an avant-garde of recollection, of memory, of the invisible, of emptiness and of death.

Death, with it ends this initially innocent peeking through a window. Because that window hides many gloomy mysteries. The window awakens dread and a sense of that which is 'beyond'. And the absence of children gives the impression that the children have already lived out their lives, that they have died, and that it is only through this fact of their *having died*—through death—that this classroom becomes filled with recollections, and that only then do these recollections start to live and acquire a mysterious spiritual power. Then, there is nothing greater than them, nothing stronger . . .

Recently, after more than 10 years, during which *Dead Class* circumnavigated the entire world, I became conscious of yet another aspect of this fascination with looking 'through the window'. Visuality, as a precondition of perception, this beholding 'from outside', this presumptuous material 'tactility', this pedantic verifiability, all evoked in me the opposition I have described and the striving to transgress the threshold of visibility, of that apodictic and absolute precondition, that 'cable' or 'conduit', which is reputedly the only one able to guarantee 'an overview'.

The idea of *Dead Class* had its beginning precisely in this fragmentary, shameful seeing. The whole methodology of the performance functioned according to the principle of

the beholding (is this even a beholding?) of
that which hermetically veiled by an imper-
meable shell— that renowned form, which
has for millennia arrogated to itself the pre-
tension to be the content and the essence of a
work. It is the highest tactlessness not to be
satisfied with this 'outside', to strive, offen-
sively, to go around it, to try to observe it
otherwise, from 'inside', to spy into it. This is
not easy. The price that one pays for this is a
meeting with death.

A LATE KADDISH

Piotr Kłoczowski

For Richard Schechner, friend of Jan Kott, Tadeusz Kantor and Jerzy Grotowski

Jan Kott's *Kaddish: Pages on Tadeusz Kantor* is the last book published during his lifetime. These pages on Tadeusz Kantor remain, to this day, one of the most poignant descriptions of what might be called 'the experience of Kantor'. Hidden within them is a fundamental philosophical question: What can save the memory of the the-atre—the image or the Logos/Word? What can save Tadeusz Kantor's Theatre of Death? Kott's answer, hidden in his *Kaddish*, is as follows: the theatre of Kantor can be saved in its essence, in its meaning, only by the Word, the Logos. This is a biblical answer. I would like to begin with Kott. Three Poles are spoken of as having left a signifi-cant mark on the territory of theatre, in the second half of the twentieth century: Tadeusz Kantor, Jerzy Grotowski and Jan Kott.

Kott is the author of *Shakespeare Our Contemporary*—a key book, from the beginning of the 1960s till today. It suffices to remember the influence that this book had on Peter Brook, on Giorgio Strehler . . . . When, in 2013, shortly before his sudden death, Patrice Chereau was beginning his work on *As You Like It,* at Luc Bondy's Odeon, he searched for the second volume of *Shakespeare Our Contemporary*—namely, *The Gender of Rosalind.*

From the middle of the 1960s, Jan Kott was an emigrant; he lectured at State University of New York at Stony Brook on Long Island and, later, held a permanent residency at the Getty Foundation in Santa Monica, California. He saw *Wielopole, Wielopole* and *The Dead Class* for the first time in Manhattan, at the La MaMa theatre. Later, he travelled after Kantor everywhere, in America and in Europe. This was the 1980s, and his initiation into Kantor's Theatre of Death:

> I saw Kantor's performances in Nancy, in Florence, in Berlin and in New York's La MaMa. I even met some devoted viewers of this theatre, who wandered

after Kantor like ducks after a wagon or,
rather, like seagulls after a ship. Clearly,
this theatre provides some nourishment,
even if bitter, though it is different from
the wide world's other shows. Perhaps it
is like this also because Kantor—like
only a few artists of our time—has
translated into theatrical signs a forgotten memory, which is present in every
one of us like a badly healed wound.
And maybe in this, precisely, lies the
cathartic role of Kantor/Charon, who
restores the dead.

In Kott's *Kaddish*, we find from the start this
private, almost intimate, side; as if Kantor
allowed Kott to recognize his Jewish roots and
fate. This was one of those extraordinary experi-
ences, where life and art interpenetrate. This was,
for Kott, a real revelation.

When I proposed to Kott to collect these
occasional and dispersed texts about Kantor, I
came upon a moving description of something
that happened years before, at the beginning of
the 1960s in Paris, in the Marais quarter, on the
rue des Rosiers. A young orthodox Jew
approached Kott and asked him if he had said
Kaddish for his father. Kaddish or, in other

words, the prayer for the deceased. Kott ends this reminiscence with the question: In which other city will a stranger approach me and ask if I have said Kaddish for my father? It seems to me that this is the true beginning of *Kaddish: Pages on Tadeusz Kantor*.

I remember that Kott decidedly did not want *Kaddish* to contain photos from performances. He said that such photographs are the true death of theatre. To recall a well-known sentence from Susan Sontag's book *On Photography*: 'To possess the world in the form of images is, precisely, to reexperience the unreality and remoteness of the real.'[1]

He wanted solely photographs of objects, taken in the context of cataloguing and not for artistic ends. This choice reflected Kott's consideration for the cult of craftsmanship in Kantor. Claude Lévi-Strauss thought the craftsman to be the best form of mediation between us and the real world. This was very close to Kantor's heart. Carpenters, blacksmiths and toolmakers were invaluable to Kantor. When he was preparing *Wielopole, Wielopole* in Florence, he brought

---

1 Susan Sontag, 'The Image-World' in *On Photography* (London: Penguin, 2019[1977]), pp. 164–96; here, p. 177.

them over from Krakow. The Italians offered him all their electronic equipment, the most modern available in that era; Kantor, however, always angrily refused. When I was preparing *Kaddish*, this madness in which we live today, of digitalizing the entire world, did not yet exist. These small photographs from the theatre's inventory, used in the first edition of the book—and also in the French, Italian and even Japanese publications—made of this small work a sort of Sebaldian book. It is worth recalling that Sebald was, at the time, working on *The Rings of Saturn*. The relationship between Kantor and Sebald was, in any case, noticed earlier by Georges Banu.

Kott wrote to me that Susan Sontag, who was a close friend of his, was enchanted by this little book. She read it in French and dreamt of an American edition. She told Kott that *Kaddish* is very close to the work of Roland Barthes, especially the pages dedicated to a photograph of his mother, discovered only after her death, in the second part of *Camera Lucida*. For Sontag, this was the Barthes of his last lectures at the Collège de France, in 1978–80, dedicated to the preparation of the novel, the patron of which was, for Barthes, Proust himself. These lectures, together with the second part of *Camera Lucida*, show

Barthes the *antimoderne*, to use the formula from Antoine Compagnon's famous book, of which Barthes is one of the heroes. To this constellation we can today add the last book by Sontag dedicated to photography, *Regarding the Pain of Others*, which Sontag herself describes as 'conservative critique': 'I call this argument conservative because it is the *sense* of reality that is eroded. There is still a reality that exists independent of the attempts to weaken its authority. The argument is in fact a defense of reality and the imperiled standards for responding more fully to it.'[2]

Jan Kott, Roland Barthes, Susan Sontag and Tadeusz Kantor—four *antimodernes* of the end of the twentieth century! Or, to put it otherwise, four splendid figures of Edward W. Said's *late style*.

There is still one more, very important, circumstance: when I was preparing this book in 1976, Maria Stangret, Kantor's wife, showed me, in their apartment in Krakow, a small box in which Kantor kept a few photos—prints of an epoch—along with several pages of typescript. She told me that this was Kantor's greatest, most

2 Susan Sontag, *Regarding the Pain of Others* (London: Penguin, 2004), p. 97.

intimate treasure. Back then, the box was still very private, truly intimate, hidden, not destined to be shown. Stangret told me, in the simplest way, that the whole Theatre of Death emerged from this box.

The contents of this treasure included the following photos:

> Helena Kantor née Berger, Kantor's mother;
>
> Marian Kantor, Helena Kantor and her brother Stanisław Berger (the uncle of T.K.);
>
> the parish church in Wielopole;
>
> some Austrian soldiers, the first on the left in the front row being Marian Kantor, the father of T.K. (1914);
>
> the town square in Wielopole, with uncle Stanisław in the foreground and, further back, Helena and Marian Kantor (c.1910).

Now all of this is professionally digitalized and catalogued at the *Cricoteka* in Krakow. This intimate treasure finds itself now in a different reality, in the reality of archives, outside of real life. However, I think that we should retain in memory the intimate meaning of this box, these photos, this wound. As Barthes wrote:

> I cannot reproduce the Winter Garden Photograph. It exists only for me. For

you, it would be nothing but an indiffer-
ent picture, one of the thousand mani-
festations of the 'ordinary'; it cannot in
any way constitute the visible object of a
science; it cannot establish an objectivity,
in the positive sense of the term; at most
it would interest your *studium*: period,
clothes, photogeny; but in it, for you, *no
wound*.[3]

Both in the past and today, Kantor and his
Theatre of Death move against the current of all
those recent tendencies in the field of theatre,
which neglect Memory-Mnemosyne in favour of
a liquid modernity.

And because of this, Kantor may provide
an alternative for all those who would like to step
outside the chalk circle of post-dramaturgic performance, which remains in a somewhat too-
dangerous symbiosis with the neoliberal market,
whether physical or digital, founded upon the
consumption of time and of things. Kantor sought
salvation from this development, about which
Barthes wrote at the end of *Camera Lucida*: 'when
generalized, it completely de-realizes the human

3 Roland Barthes, *Camera Lucida* (New York: Hill and
Wang, 1981), p. 73.

world of conflicts and desires, under cover of illustrating it.' From this perspective, *The Dead Class* and *Wielopole, Wielopole* are, 'the cry of anarchisms, marginalisms, and individualisms: let us abolish the images, let us save immediate Desire (desire without mediation).'[4]

In Kantor, there is a strong biblical side—a respect for that which is, for that which is given, for existence, for Being. In this he is close, for instance, to Hannah Arendt. Kantor remains as if at the opposite pole in relation to Jerzy Grotowski—that gnostic, rebellious with regard to what is given; but both remain on the side of life and Memory (Mnemosyne), not on the side of the void, the *nihil*.

4 Barthes, *Camera Lucida*, p. 118.

LIST OF ILLUSTRATIONS